5-06

England

by Susan H. Gray

Content Adviser: Professor Sherry L. Field,
Department of Social Science Education, College of Education,
The University of Georgia

Reading Adviser: Dr. Linda D. Labbo,
Department of Reading Education, College of Education,
The University of Georgia

 COMPASS POINT BOOKS

Minneapolis, Minnesota

FIRST REPORTS

Compass Point Books
3722 West 50th Street, #115
Minneapolis, MN 55410

Visit Compass Point Books on the Internet at *www.compasspointbooks.com* or e-mail your request to *custserv@compasspointbooks.com*.

Cover: Tower Bridge in London, England

Photographs ©: Photo Network/Paul Thompson, cover; Photo Network/Lee L. Waldman, 4; XNR Productions, Inc., 5; TRIP/K. McLaren, 6; TRIP/C. Kapolka, 7; Photo Network/Stephen Saks, 8, 9, 22, 25 (inset); James P. Rowan, 10, 21, 24, 27, 28, 30, 43; Michael G. Gabridge/Visuals Unlimited, 11; TRIP/B. Gadsby, 12; Photo Network/Paul Thompson, 13, 25 (bottom), 33; Tom Till, 14; Cheryl Hogue/Visuals Unlimited, 15, 23; Hulton Getty/Archive Photos, 16, 17, 18; Reuters/POOL/Archive Photos, 19; William Weber/Visuals Unlimited, 20; TRIP/C. Wormald, 26; Roger Treadwell/Visuals Unlimited, 29; TRIP/H. Rogers, 31, 32, 34, 35, 38; TRIP/B. Crawshaw, 36; Photo Network/John Sanford, 37; Adrienne DeLiso, 39; TRIP/R. Chester, 40–41; Glenn Oliver/Visuals Unlimited, 42; Norman Owen Tomalin/Bruce Coleman, Inc., 45.

Editors: E. Russell Primm, Emily J. Dolbear, and Neal Durando
Photo Researcher: Svetlana Zhurkina
Photo Selector: Catherine Neitge
Designer: Bradfordesign, Inc.

Library of Congress Cataloging-in-Publication Data
Gray, Susan Heinrichs.
   England / by Susan H. Gray.
      p. cm. — (First reports)
   Includes bibliographical references and index.
   ISBN 0-7565-0127-X (lib. bdg.)
   1. England—Juvenile literature. [1. England.] I. Title. II. Series.
   DA27.5 .G68 2001
   942—dc21
                                                        2001001455

Table of Contents

"Hello, Chum!" 4

The Land and Water 7

England's Long History 14

The Royal Family Today 18

Homes Big and Small 21

Getting Around in England 27

Building the Chunnel 30

Special Days 33

Soldiers, Mash, Crisps, and Scones 38

The Home of Soccer 40

Glossary 44

Did You Know? 44

At a Glance 45

Important Dates 46

Want to Know More? 47

Index 48

"Hello, Chum!"

▲ A modern Englishman dressed up as a knight on horseback

"Hello, chum! Welcome to England!" You might hear this greeting if you visit England. England is part of an island called Great Britain. The other parts of Great Britain are Scotland and Wales. Along with Northern Ireland, they make up the United Kingdom.

▲ Map of England

England's capital and largest city is London. About 7 million people live in London.

▲ *Sandown Beach on the Isle of Wight*

England is about the size of North Carolina. The land is divided into thirty-four counties. One of these counties is called the Isle of Wight. It is a small island. The Isle of Wight is a good place to find dinosaur bones!

The Land and Water

The Pennine Mountains rise in northern England. Because there are many lakes there, people call this area the Lake District. Tourists visit the Lake District every year.

▲ *Dent Valley in the Pennine Mountains is good for farming.*

▲ *Sailing is popular on Lake Windermere.*

Many rivers and **plains** run through the south of England. The best-known river is the Thames. It flows through London.

In the past, an old stone bridge crossed the Thames River. It was called London Bridge. An American bought the bridge and moved it to Arizona. It is still there today. Now people in London use the Tower Bridge instead.

▲ *London's Tower Bridge*

▲ The white cliffs of Dover

The town of Dover is in southeast England. It is famous for its white cliffs. They are made of chalk. In southwest England, a rocky point juts into the sea. It is called Land's End.

Cloudy days and fog are common in England. But the famous pea-soup fogs have disappeared. Laws that prevent air pollution have helped a lot.

▲ *Fog in London*

Much of England is surrounded by water. The North Sea lies to the east. It is a wild and stormy sea. The English Channel is the name of the **waterway** in the south between England and France. The Irish Sea is on the west coast.

▲ *Dunstanburg Castle on the North Sea coast in Northumberland*

▲ *Rocks jut into the ocean on the Cornwall coast.*

With water all around, many English people like to sail. England has always had a good navy. English traders have sailed all over the world for many years.

England's Long History

People have lived in England for thousands of years. Some of the places they built are still standing.

Stonehenge is one of these places. Thousands of years ago people who lived in southern England made it. At Stonehenge, people set up huge standing stones in circles. No one knows how or why they did this. You can still visit these strange rocks today.

▲ *The circle of rocks at Stonehenge is thousands of years old.*

▲ *Hadrian's Wall was built by the Romans in northern England.*

More than 2,000 years ago, Roman soldiers attacked England. The Romans built many roads. Some are still used today.

The Romans also built a wall across northern England to keep out the Scots. They added forts and towers to strengthen the wall. Much of this wall still stands. It is called Hadrian's Wall, after the Roman ruler Hadrian.

▲ *A knight rides a horse wearing armor in about 1160.*

About 1,600 years ago, people came to England
from Germany. Some were called Angles because
they came from a place called Angeln. So many

▲ *Henry VI as an adult*

Angles came to England that the island people called it Angle-Land, or England.

People came to England from other places too. Some were kings. When a king died, his oldest son usually became king.

Sometimes this system did not work. For example, in 1422, King Henry V died and left his son, Henry VI, to rule. But the young boy was only nine months old! His uncles came to England to take over instead.

The Royal Family Today

England still has a royal family. The queen or king reads all the important new laws. The royal family

▲ *Queen Elizabeth II with her two oldest children, Charles and Anne, her husband, Philip, and her mother, Elizabeth, at Buckingham Palace in 1953*

▲ *Prince Charles meets pipers during a festival.*

entertains important visitors. They talk about ways to help the environment. They visit sick children in hospitals. They try to set a good example.

▲ *The changing of the guard at Buckingham Palace*

The royal family has large homes and castles. Their castle in London is called Buckingham Palace. It has about 600 rooms!

Guards in bright red coats and tall bearskin hats stand at the palace gate. If you were to visit Buckingham Palace in the morning, you could watch the guards march out.

Homes Big and Small

The royal family is not the only family to have lived in a castle. Years ago, rich families built castles on the tops of hills.

The castles had high, thick walls. Outside the walls

▲ *Bodiam Castle in Sussex was built in 1385.*

were deep ditches filled with water. These ditches were called **moats**. The walls and moats kept the families safe.

▲ *Castle Howard in Yorkshire*

Over the years, many of the castles fell into ruin. Some are still standing today. People have made some of them into hotels. Now tourists can stay in rooms where the royal owners once slept.

▲ *The park at Harrogate has beautiful flower gardens.*

▲ *Many English homes have flower boxes and gardens.*

Most English houses are much smaller than castles. They usually have a small garden and flower boxes in the windows. English people love gardening. You see flowers everywhere in England.

In the country, you might see a house with a roof made of cut grass, hay, or straw. That's called a **thatch roof**. Builders cover the roof with bundles of thatch. A strong thatch roof keeps out the rain.

◀ *Thatching a roof in Devon*

▲ *This cottage in Somerset has a thatch roof.*

Many famous writers were born in England. For example, A. A. Milne wrote the Winnie the Pooh stories. Beatrix Potter wrote the story of Peter Rabbit. *Alice in Wonderland* was written by Lewis Carroll. Although none of these people are still alive, you can visit their homes.

▲ *Beatrix Potter's house is in the Lake District near Sawrey.*

Getting Around in England

▲ *One of London's famous red double-decker buses*

In England, most people travel by car or train. In big cities, people also get around on **double-decker buses**. A double-decker bus has an upstairs and a downstairs.

In London, police officers direct the busy traffic. The officers are called bobbies. That's because the man who started the London police was Sir Robert Peel—or Bobby for short.

In London, people often use the subway. This is a speedy, underground train that runs through tunnels

▲ Police officers are often called bobbies.

▲ *Trains come and go from Kings Cross Station in London.*

below the city. It is sometimes called the tube because the tunnels look like big tubes.

People can take the train from cities to small towns. Trains go almost everywhere in England. They even go under the sea all the way to France!

Building the Chunnel

It has always been hard to go from England to France. Many people cross the English Channel by boat. Going by boat is slow, and sometimes the waves make people seasick. You can also fly, but this is more expensive.

▲ *A ferry crossing the English Channel*

▲ *Travelers taking their cars to France through the Channel Tunnel board a train.*

For years, people talked about digging a tunnel from England to France. Then travelers could take a train across the channel. But there were many questions. Who would dig the tunnel? How deep should it go? Who would pay for it?

Finally, Britain and France made an agreement. Big machines started to dig the tunnel. They started in England and in France. Far below the seafloor, the machines met in the tunnel they made together. Then workers built train tracks in the tunnel.

In 1994, the tunnel was finished. Now trains zip between England and France in thirty-five minutes. They run 150 feet (46 meters) below the seafloor. The tunnel is called the Channel Tunnel or the "Chunnel."

▲ *Inside a Channel Tunnel train*

▲ *A child stands beside a Guy Fawkes dummy.*

The English celebrate many holidays. On November 5, they celebrate Guy Fawkes Day.

Guy Fawkes lived 400 years ago. Guy Fawkes did not like the government or the king. He planned to blow up the king and the Houses of **Parliament**. He was caught before anything happened, on November 5. Today the English celebrate Guy Fawkes Day with **bonfires** and fireworks.

▲ *A bonfire burns the Guy Fawkes dummy.*

▲ *Fireworks explode over Parliament and the famous clock called Big Ben.*

Christmas Day is celebrated on December 25. The next day—Boxing Day—is also a holiday. Years ago, rich families gave boxes of gifts to their servants on this day.

Today most people do not have servants. So, on Boxing Day, they give gifts to people who deliver the mail or take away the trash.

▲ *The River Thames flows through London.*

In London, many graceful swans glide along the Thames River. In the third week in July, people in London enjoy Swan Upping week.

During Swan Upping, people row boats up the river. They cry "All Up!" when they see baby swans.

▲ *Weighing a baby swan during Swan Upping*

They count them and gently pick them up. Then
they weigh the little swans and check their health.
After that, they put them back in the river. Swan
Upping week lets everyone know how the swans
are doing.

Soldiers, Mash, Crisps, and Scones

The English call their dishes by clever names. English children eat porridge, or oatmeal, for breakfast. Or they have eggs and soldiers—small slices of toast. For a snack, they might eat chips (french fries) or crisps (chips).

▲ *A girl enjoys fish and chips.*

▲ *An English tea shop*

At lunch, children enjoy bangers and mash (sausage and mashed potatoes). They might also have *scones* (rolls) with jam. For dessert they might have *biscuits* (cookies). Everyone usually drinks tea with meals.

Another favorite food is called shepherd's pie. It is a dish made of meat, gravy, vegetables, and mashed potatoes. One helping of shepherd's pie makes a lovely meal!

The Home of Soccer

For fun, many English boys and girls play soccer. They call it "football."

The English invented the game in the 1800s.

Soccer teams formed all over the country. Then sailors and traders taught the game of soccer to people in other countries.

Now soccer is played in more than 200 countries. It is the most popular game in the world.

In England, soccer is called football.

▲ *A cricket match can last for several days.*

Children and grown-ups also play cricket. Cricket teams bowl balls, bat them, and score runs. A cricket match may go on for days. Cricket teams may score hundreds of runs.

▲ *St. James's Park is in front of Whitehall government offices.*

If you visit England, you will learn more about this interesting country. Then as you leave, you might say, "Cheerio! I enjoyed my visit to England."

Glossary

bonfires—large outdoor fires

double-decker buses—buses with an upstairs and a downstairs

moats—deep, wide ditches around castles to prevent attacks

Parliament—the British government

plains—flat land

thatch roof—a roof made of cut straw, hay, or grass

waterway—a body of water on which ships travel

Did You Know?

- In England, people drive automobiles on the left side of the road.

- Oxford and Cambridge, two of the world's most famous universities, are both in England.

- The British Library in London has 18 million printed books and 8 million stamp-related items.

- The most popular tourist attraction in London is Madame Tussaud's Waxworks museum.

At a Glance

Official name: England (The official name of the country that England is a part of is the United Kingdom of Great Britain and Northern Ireland.)

Capital: London (also the capital of the United Kingdom)

Official language: English

National song: "God Save the Queen (or King)"

Area: 50,352 square miles (130,412 square kilometers)

Highest point: Scafell Pike, 3,210 feet (979 meters)

Lowest point: Great Holme Fen, –9 feet (–2.7 meters)

Population: 49,208,000 (2000 estimate)

Head of government: Prime minister

Money: Pound

Important Dates

55 B.C.	Julius Caesar explores what is now England.
1066	The Normans invade England, and William the Conqueror becomes the king of England.
1337	France and England fight in the Hundred Years' War.
1509	King Henry VIII becomes king of England.
1529–1536	The Church of England is created.
1558	Elizabeth I becomes queen of England.
1783	England loses the Revolutionary War.
1940	Winston Churchill is elected prime minister of England.
1952	Elizabeth II becomes queen of England.
1979	Margaret Thatcher is elected prime minister and becomes the first woman to hold the office.
1994	A railroad tunnel under the English Channel opens.

Want to Know More?

At the Library

Aliki. *William Shakespeare and the Globe*. New York: HarperCollins Juvenile, 1999.

Stanley, Diane. *Good Queen Bess: The Story of Elizabeth I of England*. New York: William Morrow, 2001.

Weinberger, Kimberly. *Princess Diana: Forever in Our Hearts*. New York: Scholastic, 1998.

On the Web

The British Monarchy

http://www.royal.gov.uk

For a guide to the royal rulers of Great Britain

Castles of Britain

http://www.castles-of-britain.com

For information about castles in Great Britain

Museum of the History of Science

http://www.mhs.ox.ac.uk

For an online tour of this historic museum at Oxford University

Through the Mail

British Information Services

845 Third Avenue

New York, NY 10022

To get information from the office of the British Embassy

On the Road

The Yale Center for British Art

1080 Chapel Street

New Haven, CT 06510

203/432-2800

To view a large collection of English paintings, prints, drawings, books, and sculpture

Index

Boxing Day, 35
Buckingham Palace, 20
Carroll, Lewis, 26
castles, 21–23
Channel Tunnel, 30–32
chips, 38
Christmas Day, 35
cricket, 42
double-decker buses, 27
Dover, 10
English Channel, 12, 30
gardens, 24
Great Britain, 4
guards, 20
Guy Fawkes Day, 33, 34
Hadrian's Wall, 15
Henry V, king of England,
    17
houses, 24–25
Irish Sea, 12–13
Isle of Wight, 6
kings, 17, 18
Lake District, 7
London, 5, 8
London Bridge, 8

Milne, A. A., 26
moats, 22
navy, 13
North Sea, 12
Northern Ireland, 4
Pennine Mountains, 7
police officers, 28
pollution, 10
Potter, Beatrix, 26
public transit, 27, 28–32
queens, 18
rivers, 7–8
roads, 15
Roman invasion, 15
royal family, 18–20
scones, 39
Scotland, 4
soccer, 40–41
Stonehenge, 14
subway system, 28–29
tea, 39
Thames River, 8, 36
tourism, 7, 23
trains, 28–29
Wales, 4

About the Author

Susan H. Gray holds bachelor's and master's degrees in zoology from the University of Arkansas in Fayetteville. She has taught classes in general biology, human anatomy, and physiology. She has also worked as a fresh-water biologist and scientific illustrator. In her twenty years as a writer, Susan H. Gray has covered many topics and written a variety of science books for children.